Family Pets

by Lola M. Schaefer

Consulting Editor: Gail Saunders-Smith, Ph.D.

Consultant: Phyllis Edelbrock, First-Grade Teacher,
University Place School District, Washington

Pebble Books

an imprint of Capstone Press
Mankato, Minnesota

Pebble Books are published by Capstone Press
818 North Willow Street, Mankato, Minnesota 56001
http://www.capstone-press.com

Library of Congress Cataloging-in-Publication Data
Schaefer, Lola M., 1950–
    Family pets/by Lola M. Schaefer.
    p. cm.—(Families)
    Includes bibliographical references and index.
    Summary: In simple text and illustrations, describes a variety of pets including
cats, fish, rabbits, dogs, and ponies.
    ISBN 0-7368-0255-X
    1. Pets—Juvenile literature. [1. Pets.] I. Title. II. Series: Schaefer, Lola M.,
1950–   Families.
S416.2.S32   1999
636.088'7—dc21

                                      98-46079
                                      CIP
                                      AC

Note to Parents and Teachers

The Families series supports national social studies standards for
units related to identifying family members and their roles in the
family. This book describes and illustrates a variety of family pets.
The photographs support emergent readers in understanding the
text. The repetition of words and phrases helps emergent readers
learn new words. This book also introduces emergent readers to
subject-specific vocabulary words, which are defined in the Words
to Know section. Descriptive language and adjectives are used in
the text. Emergent readers may need assistance to read some words
and to use the Table of Contents, Words to Know, Read More,
Internet Sites, and Index/Word List sections of the book.

2

Table of Contents

Guinea pigs are
furry pets.

Rabbits are fluffy pets.

Dogs are playful pets.

Ponies are big pets.

Cats are soft pets.

Turtles are hard pets.

Fish are wet pets.

Birds are singing pets.

Pets are good friends.

Words to Know

guinea pig—a small animal with smooth fur, short ears, and a short tail

hard—firm and solid

pet—a tame animal kept for company

playful—frisky and willing to play

pony—a small horse

soft—smooth and gentle to touch

wet—covered with liquid

Read More

Driscoll, Laura. *All about Dogs and Puppies.* All Aboard Books. New York: Grosset & Dunlap, 1998.

Hansen, Ann Larkin. *Birds.* Popular Pet Care. Minneapolis: Abdo & Daughters, 1997.

Morley, Christine and Carole Orbell. *Me and My Pet Fish.* Chicago: World Book, 1997.

Scott, Carey. *Kittens.* New York: DK Publishing, 1997.

Internet Sites

Complete Hamster Site
http://www.hamsters.co.uk/index2.htm

Healthy Pets
http://www.healthypet.com

Pet Home Page
http://www.pet.com

Index/Word List

big, 11	friends, 21	ponies, 11
birds, 19	furry, 5	rabbits, 7
cats, 13	good, 21	singing, 19
dogs, 9	guinea pigs, 5	soft, 13
fish, 17	hard, 15	turtles, 15
fluffy, 7	playful, 9	wet, 17

Word Count: 37
Early-Intervention Level: 4

Editorial Credits
Mari C. Schuh, editor; Steve Weil/Tandem Design, cover designer and illustrator;
   Kimberly Danger, photo researcher

Photo Credits
Brian Beck, 1
Cheryl R. Richter, cover
David F. Clobes, 8, 16
Dusty L. Perin, 10
Photo Network/Myrleen Cate, 20
Rainbow/Dan McCoy, 18
Stephen Simpson/FPG International LLC, 4
The Stock Market/Ariel Skelley, 14
Transparencies, Inc./Jane Faircloth, 12
Unicorn Stock Photos/Chris Boylan, 6

Special thanks to Joy Allison, Lori Hollenback, and Penny McCarthy, first-grade
teachers at Evergreen Primary in University Place, Washington, for reviewing the
books in the Families series.